If you had inadvertently telephoned Whitehall 7171 in 1940, you might have been surprised to find you had been given access to one of the most secret installations of the war, the Cabinet War Rooms.

This well-hidden site, whose location and purpose were known to none but the most privileged – and certainly not to the German High Command – operated round the clock every day of the year, from the beginning to the end of the Second World War. Few outsiders were allowed to pass the armed guards who kept constant watch on its entrances, buried deep in Whitehall's cellars, but anyone who did might have found the most remarkable concentration of Great Britain's senior political and military figures ever imaginable in one place at one time. It was here Winston Churchill, his War Cabinet, the heads of the three branches of the Armed Services and the top echelons of military intelligence and planning found shelter to work undisturbed by the heavy bombing raids which made daily life so difficult above ground.

Today the Imperial War Museum is pleased to welcome you to the Cabinet War Rooms without passes or armed guards, and to let you into the secret everyday life of those who kept Britain's government and war machine working throughout the conflict. As you walk through the rooms try to think not only of the well-known personalities of those times, but also of the many unsung people who toiled here, firm in the conviction that peace would one day return to the bombed-out streets above.

President George W Bush in the War Cabinet Room.

Philip Reed
Director
Cabinet War Rooms

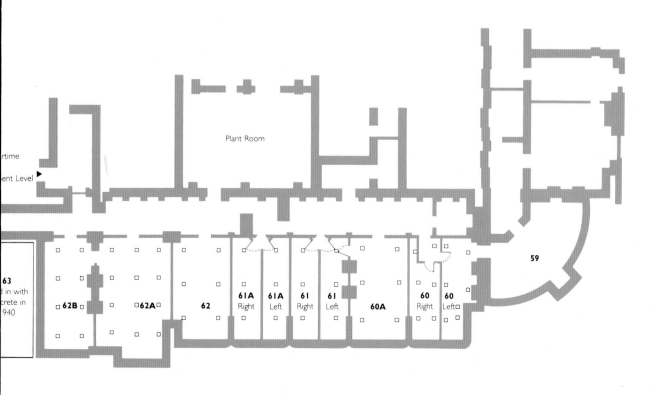

The Cabinet War Rooms and the Second World War

1938	15 June	Site for a Central War Room agreed.	
	September	Rooms staffed during crisis.	Munich Crisis.
1939	27 August	Central Map Room comes into use.	
	3 September		Britain declares war on Germany.
	21 October	First Cabinet meeting in the War Rooms, under Neville Chamberlain.	
	29 December	Name 'Central War Room' changed to 'Cabinet War Room'.	
1940	10 May		Germany invades the Netherlands. Winston Churchill becomes Prime Minister.
	May	Churchill visits the Cabinet War Rooms and declares 'This is the room from which I'll direct the war.'	
	25 May–4 June		Dunkirk evacuation.
	10 July–31 October		Battle of Britain.
	27 July	Room 65A assigned to Churchill as combined office and bedroom.	
	29 July	Cabinet meeting in War Rooms (under Winston Churchill). Advanced Headquarters Home Forces functioning in Cabinet War Rooms.	
	7 September		London Blitz begins.
	11 September	Churchill makes first broadcast from Cabinet War Rooms.	
	26 September	Near-miss for Cabinet War Rooms when bomb hits Clive Steps, by present day entrance.	
	September–December	Frequent Cabinet meetings in War Rooms. Protective slab constructed.	
	December	No. 10 Annexe in New Public Offices Great George Street ready for occupation.	
1941	10 May		Period of heaviest air raids on London ends.
	Spring	Advanced Headquarters Home Forces moves out of Cabinet War Rooms.	
	22 June		Germany invades Soviet Union.
	8 December		Britain and United States declare war on Japan.
1942	October		Allied success in North Africa at Battle of El Alamein.
1943	January		German retreat from Soviet Union begins.
	10 July		Allied invasion of Sicily.
	July		Transatlantic Telephone Room ready for use.
	3 September		Allied invasion of Italy.
1944	6 June		D-Day: Allied invasion of North-West Europe.
	13 June		First V-1 falls on London.
	19 June–9 September	All Cabinet meetings held in War Rooms.	
	8 September		First V-2 falls on London.
1945	9 January–28 March	Most Cabinet meetings held in War Rooms.	
	28 March	Last Cabinet meeting in the War Rooms.	Last V-2 falls on London.
	8 May		VE Day: end of Second World War in Europe.
	27 July		Clement Attlee becomes Prime Minister.
	15 August		VJ Day marks end of war against Japan.
	16 August	Central Map Room closes.	

The Origins of the Cabinet War Rooms

Among the many new weapons and threats which the First World War introduced to mankind was the aerial bombardment of cities: the attempt to destroy centres of commerce, civilian life and, above all, government, which until then had been remote from the physical impact of conflict. The bombing of undefended cities was practised during the First World War and the Spanish Civil War, causing many civilian casualties.

The fear that cities, and particularly London, would be the first targets of an enemy conducting a war against Great Britain troubled successive British governments in the 1920s and 1930s. It seemed that the nightmare of mass slaughter of civilians and the destruction of ordered government might be realised and the question became more urgent as to how the Prime Minister, his Cabinet and the central core of the military command could be protected in the event of a war involving the European powers.

RAF planners drew a horrifying picture of 600 tons of bombs raining down on the capital, causing 200,000 casualties in just the first week of a war. Schemes for the evacuation of the Prime Minister, the Cabinet, and its administrative machinery were prepared as early as the 1920s. Numerous competing schemes were studied, costed and even constructed throughout the 1930s, among them the adaptation of basement offices and the tunnelling of deep shelters in central London and in the capital's north-west suburbs.

Eventually the concern that the public might think their leaders were deserting them persuaded the planners to look to the possibility of providing a secure 'Central War Room', nearer to the traditional home of government.

Laurence Burgis, Camp Commandant at the Cabinet War Rooms, and General Leslie Hollis, who played a crucial role in setting them up.
IWM HU 43871

The outer wall of the New Public Offices shows the solid concrete apron put in place to limit the effects of bomb blast and shell splinters in the Cabinet War Rooms below.

The site chosen was nothing grander than the basement chambers of the Office of Works' building which faced St. James's Park and Horseguards Road on one side and Great George Street on the other. Known properly as the 'New Public Offices' – so called when it was constructed at the turn of the century – but referred to throughout the war simply as 'George Street', this building offered the strongest structure of any in Whitehall and was conveniently situated between Parliament and the Prime Minister's office-residence at Number 10 Downing Street.

Work began in June 1938 on adapting these humble storage areas, ten feet below ground, to house the central core of government and a unique military information centre to serve the Prime Minister and the Chiefs of Staff of the air, naval and land forces. The events of the Munich crisis in the early autumn speeded up the process. Seen by most planners as no more than a temporary expedient, the rooms were constructed under the careful eye of Major-General Sir Hastings (later Lord) Ismay, ably assisted by Major (later Major-General Sir Leslie) Hollis, and became fully operational on 27 August 1939, exactly a week before the German invasion of Poland and Britain's declaration of war. This 'temporary' measure was to serve as the central shelter for government and the military strategists for the next six years.

As you go round the site, you will see elements of the rudimentary protection afforded to the Rooms in those early days, as well as clear signs of the additional reinforcement which was installed as the war went on and the bombs being used became more and more destructive.

The Cabinet War Rooms since 1945

With the surrender of the Japanese forces in the Far East in August 1945, the Rooms were no longer needed and, on 16 August 1945, the lights in the Central Map Room were switched off for the very first time since the start of the war and the door was locked. This room, its annexe, Churchill's office-bedroom and the Cabinet Room were then left intact and undisturbed until an announcement in Parliament in 1948 ensured their preservation as an historic site. Restricted access was subsequently possible, but few were even aware of the existence of this previously top secret installation and it was only in 1981 when the Prime Minister, Margaret Thatcher, decided that the site should be made more easily accessible that its history became more widely known.

During the next three years the Imperial War Museum and the Department of the Environment arranged for the careful preservation and restoration of the complex and made the adaptations which were necessary to give visitors an intimate view of the contents of the Rooms and the routines of life in them.

Although the uses of the Rooms, and the people who occupied them, changed during the war, in line with the exigencies of the military situation, the Museum took every care to make certain that the Rooms retained their authentic wartime appearance. All the fixtures and fittings, all the documents, maps and books that still clutter the corridors and offices, even the sign boards, the lights, the décor itself, are contemporary, and are now as they were then or have been restored to their original positions and purpose.

The Entrance

The sand bags which surround the 'bunker' entrance, through which today's visitors reach the Cabinet War Rooms, contain a mixture of sand and cement. They are a recent construction, modelled on the entrances to government installations in the area in 1939 and 1940. The entrance itself is also a convenient modern addition: the usual route into the Rooms during the war was down carefully guarded stairs leading from the Government offices in the building above.

The 'sand-bagged' entrance to the Cabinet War Rooms today.

The Introductory Gallery

The first part of the Rooms comprises what must once have been the least imposing part of the site. Used until after the war as coal bunkers, the alcoves now house displays relating to the background history of the war. Panoramas of London's horizon, almost obscured by the smoke of explosions, mix with smaller scale, more human scenes of individual suffering and courage.

A display case houses the map on which Churchill charted the division of Europe in 1945, alongside the Rooms' wartime visitors' book and three lumps of rationed sugar, hidden for nearly forty years.

Visitors view a display in the Introductory Gallery.

The Cabinet Room

Beyond the foyer a new entrance leads to the room once occupied by General Hollis. One wall has been opened up to allow visitors a unique view of the Cabinet Room. This was the inner sanctum of British government, the room used for meetings of the Prime Minister, a select few ministers and advisers of his War Cabinet and his Chiefs of Staff.

Neville Chamberlain, Prime Minister at the outbreak of the Second World War, held only one Cabinet meeting in this room, on 21 October 1939. Under Winston Churchill, who succeeded Chamberlain as Prime Minister on 10 May 1940, 115 Cabinet meetings, roughly one in ten of all the War Cabinet meetings, were held here.

Churchill occupied the large wooden seat at the far side of the room and, with his Deputy Prime Minister and Leader of the Labour Party, Clement Attlee, on his left, presided over a coalition of ministers drawn from all sides of Parliament. His Cabinet usually consisted of no more than eight ministers, but he was assisted at meetings by civilian and military advisers. The room was also used frequently by the Defence Committee, which, in the first years of the war, served as Churchill's principal instrument for conducting the war, bringing together specific ministers and the Chiefs of Staff of the armed forces. They would occupy the three seats in the central 'well' of the tables. The Chiefs of Staff would also use the Cabinet Room for their own meetings.

Cabinet meetings could start and finish at any time of day or night. Churchill, who was famed for retiring late, occasionally called meetings here during the evening bombing raids of 1940 and 1941 and sometimes brought them to a close long after midnight.

The clocks in the Cabinet Room have been set at 16·58 and the tables have been prepared as they were for a Cabinet meeting so that visitors can transport themselves in their imagination to the meeting which began at 5.00 pm on 15 October 1940. It was during the preceding night that a lucky strike by a German bomb seriously damaged Number 10 Downing Street and convinced Churchill that it was, after all, more sensible to use his underground headquarters for meetings which were likely to be interrupted by bombing raids.

The Cabinet Room. In front of Churchill's seat is the red box which, full of State papers, always accompanied him. The room's red girders were there to support the ceiling if the building above collapsed. The coloured lights over the door showed whether an air raid was in progress or not.

The Cabinet and the Chiefs of Staff

In the parliamentary democracy of Great Britain the power to legislate rests with the joint Houses of Parliament, that is the Lords and the Commons. In fact, policy is set not only by the government, but more particularly by the Prime Minister and his principal ministers meeting together, as equals, as the Cabinet.

It is the Cabinet which determines the overall national policy in respect of home and foreign affairs, draws up the legislative programme for a government's current term of office and co-ordinates the work of the various government departments which put policy into practice. Because of the complexities of financial, social and defence matters, it passes much of the responsibility for policy formulation on to committees which then report their findings to the Cabinet for final approval.

A 'Cabinet Secretariat', comprising the country's most senior civil servant, the Cabinet Secretary, and a hierarchy of other civil servants assisting him, attends every Cabinet meeting and keeps the record of each of their proceedings, circulating the minutes to all the participants and taking action as necessary. In wartime the equal importance of civilian and military matters led Churchill effectively to divide the post of Cabinet Secretary between General Sir Hastings Ismay, who, as Deputy Secretary (Military), was responsible for implementing all military related decisions, and Sir Edward (later Lord) Bridges, who looked after the non-military aspects of meetings.

In 1940 Churchill took on the office not only of Prime Minister, but also that of Minister of Defence. He did not create an actual Ministry of Defence, but used instead that part of the War Cabinet Secretariat which was headed by Ismay and Colonel Hollis, and a new body called the Defence Committee. This brought together service ministers and the Chiefs of Staff under Churchill's direction and enabled him to translate decisions into action more quickly.

Members of the Defence Committee at 10 Downing Street in 1941.
IWM HU 3207

The Chiefs of Staff Committee, which included the heads of the Army, Navy and Air Force, as well as General Ismay in his role as the Minister of Defence's Chief Staff Officer, was chaired nominally by the Prime Minister, but in fact by his appointee, and met to discuss overall strategy, and also to focus on immediate operational problems. A sub-committee, known as the Joint Planning Staff, comprised three sections for Strategical, Executive and Future Operational Planning. Another subordinate body, the Joint Intelligence Staff, brought together representatives of the three services' intelligence directorates, the Foreign Office and the Ministry of Economic Warfare, as well as an Intelligence Section (Operations) which supplied information to commanders and planners about areas likely to become the scene of operations.

All of these bodies were housed at some time in, and operated from, the Cabinet War Rooms. There was certainly the risk of a heavy toll on the military planning capacity of the government in the event of the Rooms' destruction in an air raid, but decision making based on sound intelligence and the broadest possible consultation benefited from such a concentration of interlocking resources.

Churchill's War Cabinet at 10 Downing Street 1941. Left to right, standing: Arthur Greenwood, Ernest Bevin, Lord Beaverbrook, Sir Kingsley Wood; seated: Sir John Anderson, Winston Churchill, Clement Attlee, Anthony Eden.
CENTRAL PRESS

The Dock

Known unaffectionately as 'the dock' by those obliged to occupy the area, another floor lies beneath a trap door in the passage beyond the room from which the Cabinet Room is viewed. In this sub-basement, which extends the full length and breadth of the building, were dormitories for the typists, clerks, administrators and others, including Churchill's butler and his valet, who worked in the floors above the Cabinet War Rooms. There was even cramped office accommodation for the ever-expanding number of staff who needed to work in a sheltered area.

Wrapped modestly in all-enveloping dressing gowns, dozens traipsed nightly down the slatted staircase, carrying their sheets to any free bed that could be found in the inhospitable dock. Most of the doorways were no more than four feet high and led into rooms with concrete floors and bare brick walls. The air conditioning, which was added to the Cabinet War Rooms as something of an afterthought, was never up to coping with the heat and humidity generated in the dock and, as its yellow trunking further reduced the height of the rooms, it was often seen as being no more than a painful obstacle.

Though there were chemical toilets there, those who slept in the sub-basement tell of the long and embarrassing trek through two floors of the building above to follow the call of nature, shadowed much of the way by one of the every-wary Marines who guarded the Cabinet Room. Many preferred to go home and risk the dangers of the air raids and the almost impenetrable dark of the black-out to squeezing into this underground den for the night.

A passage in the sub-basement or 'dock'. IWM MH 533

A Shelter from the World Outside

The main corridor in the Cabinet War Rooms.

Mr. George Rance adjusts the weather indicator.
IWM F 1338

The thick red girders, so evident in the Cabinet Room and elsewhere in the complex, were added to supplement the crude system of rough wooden piers installed in 1938. Their girth and weighty appearance almost certainly added to the mistaken belief in the site's impregnability.

No bombs ever truly tested the site's defences – though over a hundred and forty had fallen in the vicinity of Whitehall by February 1941 alone – and the people who worked here would have heard little of the wailing sirens, the drone of enemy bombers or the thunder of anti-aircraft guns, until they surfaced, often startled to find that day was now night and sunshine had been replaced by rain.

Those in the Cabinet Room itself would have the silent messages of the lights over the doorway to advise them of an air raid in progress. In the corridor outside the Cabinet Room others had a small, but quite distinctive bell to advise them that it was unwise to go above ground, while the sign put up by the ubiquitous Mr. George Rance, the civilian representative of the Ministry of Works and the all-provider of the complex, kept them informed of the weather outside. Those working in the Rooms, however, were accustomed to Mr. Rance's efforts to sustain a happy atmosphere and knew that his 'windy' sign really meant that an air raid was taking place outside.

The 'Slab'

The original concept of an underground shelter for the machinery of government envisaged a location which should be well concealed and 'bomb-proof', or at least capable of withstanding the impact of a semi-armour piercing 500-pound bomb. It was only after the Cabinet had already held frequent meetings here that the Prime Minister, who thought the site perfectly safe, discovered that in fact it came nowhere near meeting requirements and he demanded that measures be taken to improve the protection given to the Cabinet and other rooms.

In late 1940, those working in the offices above were obliged to vacate them so that work could begin on the insertion of a new protective layer in the shape of a three foot reinforced concrete slab.

The site still scarcely met the criteria which even the most optimistic ballistics experts said would be necessary to avoid the total collapse of the building under the pressure of anything heavier than 500 pounds – and as the war went on, bombs of 1700 and 1800 pounds became quite common. But Churchill stuck doggedly to his insistence on staying in central London and keeping all senior ministers and military commanders in one location, observing that, statistically, the likelihood of a bomb scoring a direct and devastating hit was minimal. Most who worked here continued to do so ignorant of the arguments and of the structure's shortcomings.

Demands from the ever swelling throng occupying the offices in the rest of the building at this level, however, made it necessary to vacate more and more precious ground floor accommodation so that the 'slab' could be extended, until it covered, as it still does, three-quarters of the whole building at the level above. A cross-section of this slab and its constituent parts can be seen in Room 59 at the end of the corridor.

The Main Corridor

The Cabinet War Rooms formed the most secret portion of a maze of tiny chambers which lay under the New Public Offices. Access to each of the principal rooms was through doors off a long corridor, which has been retained and from which visitors can gain a brief preview of the rooms themselves.

The corridor also reveals, through a variety of features – the gas filter levers, the rifle racks for use by staff in the event of close attack, the heavy sealed door of the mess room – something of the fear which beset everyone in Great Britain throughout the second half of 1940 and even early 1941: the fear of imminent invasion.

The board in the main corridor lists warning signals in use in the Cabinet War Rooms.

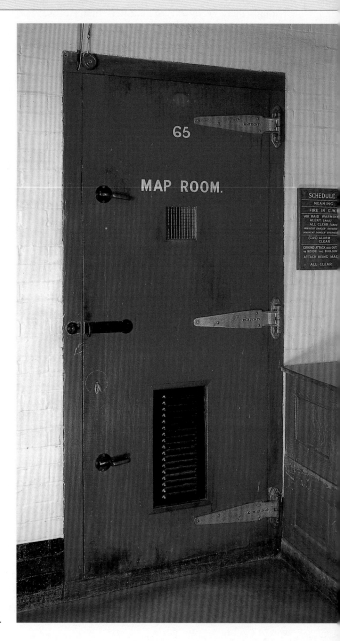

The door to the Map Room.

A small, armed garrison of Royal Marines which manned the site provided the principal protection, guarding the Cabinet Room entrance and all the underground entrances and exits to the site itself, against the sudden arrival of enemy airborne forces. The likelihood is, however, that they would not have been able to resist for long, even with the help of 'Rance's Guard', a small group of former Grenadier guardsmen, no longer fit for more active service.

The gun racks about the corridor and offices would have been filled with rifles, readily available to anyone working there to defend himself with in the case of emergency. Strict regulations covering such emergencies were posted all about the rooms.

The heavy steel doors and their solid locking levers were there to delay any possible seepage of water and gas and the incursion of armed personnel, but they would almost certainly have given only limited protection. The defensive measures were brave, though, realistically, rudimentary. Fortunately the true significance of the site does not feature in any known German wartime document, implying that the enemy did not know or perhaps would never have considered believable the converted cellar bastion which sheltered the central core of the British military and civilian hierarchy.

The Blitz

The word 'Blitz' is German for lightning and was originally used to describe the rapid enemy advance into Poland in September 1939, before being applied by the British press to the tempest of bombing raids on London and other British cities in 1940 and 1941.

Concentrated direct bombing of industrial targets and civilian centres began on 7 September 1940 with heavy raids on London. The scale of attack rapidly escalated, as the German Air Force dropped 5,300 tons of high explosives on the capital in twenty-four nights in September alone. In their effort to 'soften up' the British population and to destroy their morale before the planned invasion, German planes extended their targets to include the major coastal ports and centres of production and supply.

The infamous raid of 14 November 1940 on Coventry brought a still worse twist to the campaign when 500 German bombers dropped 500 tons of explosives and nearly 900 incendiary bombs in ten hours of unrelenting bombardment, a tactic later emulated on an even greater scale by the RAF in their attacks on German cities.

The British population had been forewarned in September 1939 that air attacks on cities were likely and civil defence preparations had been started some time before, both on a national and a local level. Simple corrugated steel Anderson shelters, covered over by earth, were dug into gardens up and down the country. Larger civic shelters built of brick and concrete were erected in British towns and a blackout was rigorously enforced after darkness.

Soon the night raids became so frequent that they were practically continuous and many people, tired of repeatedly interrupting their sleep to go back and forth to the street shelters, virtually took up residence in a particular one, giving rise to a new spirit of solidarity and community, though this was occasionally tempered with rival territorial claims. Londoners took what seemed to them an obvious and sensible solution to the problem and moved down in their thousands into the 'Tube' stations. At first actively discouraged by the government, this popular action held sway and it was a common sight for a

Blast damage in an office in 10 Downing Street, 14 October 1940.
IWM F 1725

traveller on the underground in wartime London to pass through a station crowded with semi-comatose bodies and piled high with the impedimenta of domestic life.

The main air offensive against British cities diminished after May 1941 with the change of direction of the German war machine towards Russia, though sporadic and lethal raids, using increasingly larger bombs, continued for several more years.

Churchill inspecting a bomb crater close to the present entrance to the Cabinet War Rooms, 30 September 1940. IWM F 1338

The Transatlantic Telephone Room

The Transatlantic Telephone Room is on the left of the corridor. Visitors look at it through a window which has been made in the back of a former cupboard.

Like all the rooms in the complex, this originally had a more humble purpose than its wartime role. Once the store for brooms and domestic equipment, it was adapted in mid-1943 to house a particularly secret installation, the direct telephone link between the British Prime Minister and the American President.

'Sigsaly' was the code name assigned to the equipment which was developed by scientists at the American company, Bell Telephone Laboratories, and which, for the first time ever, allowed communications between the two great Allied leaders in the full confidence that their words would not be overheard by foreign powers. For several months after 'Sigsaly' was installed in July 1943, Mr. Churchill and President Roosevelt seem to have been reluctant to give up using the commercial transatlantic telephone system which was regularly tapped by the Germans.

The technology which made a secure conversation possible was a new version of the otherwise relatively easily tapped 'scrambler'. Whereas earlier versions had been fairly small and simple, 'Sigsaly', or 'X-Ray', as the London terminal was code-named, needed not only the five feet high intermediate scrambler cabinet visible in the Transatlantic Telephone Room, but also over thirty seven feet tall relay racks weighing eighty tons, seventy-two different radio frequencies, a large air-conditioned room and 30 kW of energy – just to encipher one short conversation!

This equipment was too large and too heavy to be installed in the Cabinet War Rooms and the nearest suitable spot was found in an annexe basement of Selfridges department store in Oxford Street. The partially enciphered telephone conversation was transmitted by cable from the 'hot-line' to the Selfridges site where it was finally enciphered and sent by radio waves to the President in Washington. The recipient of the call needed a similarly large and complicated installation at his end to decipher the call.

The few surviving transcripts of the conversations reveal the confidence that both the Prime Minster and the President placed in the equipment, as they exchanged ideas about some of the most secret aspects of wartime strategy and political dealings among the Allies.

Next to the telephone lay a headset which was used by Churchill's Personal Secretary in setting up the conversation, which had to be synchronised absolutely accurately to guarantee correct transmission. The headset also allowed the Personal Secretary to take notes on the contents of the conversation.

The door to the Transatlantic Telephone Room opens out on to the corridor and is a former lavatory door, its dial half turned to show the 'engaged' sign. Its presence here gave rise to the tale that the secret nature of the room's use was maintained by a general belief that it housed the only proper toilet in the site and that this was, inevitably, assigned exclusively to the Prime Minister.

The 'Sigsaly' scrambler for the transatlantic telephone connection, housed in Selfridge's basement in Oxford Street. IWM H 45346

The Transatlantic Telephone Room.

The Transatlantic Lobby

The Transatlantic Telephone Room is situated in the corner of a wide corridor now known as the Transatlantic Lobby. During the war this area was converted into three rooms to provide office and sleeping accommodation for: Clement Attlee, Leader of the Labour Party and Deputy Prime Minister; Lord Beaverbrook, a Canadian press magnate, a close friend of Churchill's and his Minister of Aircraft Production; and Anthony Eden, Churchill's Foreign Secretary in 1940.

The corridor of the Churchill Suite, known during the war years as the 'Courtyard Rooms'.

The Churchill Suite

Running off the right of the Transatlantic Lobby is the suite of rooms into which the Cabinet War Rooms expanded in 1941. This sequence of rooms, now known as the 'Churchill Suite', provided private chambers for Winston Churchill's private office staff and his wife, Clementine, as well as a dining facility for himself and 'Clemmie' and a meeting room for his Chiefs of Staff.

All of these rooms were stripped out at the end of the war and were subsequently used as low-grade storage and even as a gymnasium, until their restoration in 2003. The work of restoration was greatly assisted by a series of detailed photographs which were taken of the rooms at the end of the war. Using these, every effort was made to make the rooms resemble their original wartime format. Although most of the furnishings had to be found from government office basements, second-hand shops and the attics and garages of private individuals, some of the original room contents were kept and have been restored to their previous wartime location.

The Churchills' Private Dining Room.

Staff in the Churchill Suite

The Prime Minister was, as one might expect, accompanied by one of his private detectives wherever he went. They were given rudimentary accommodation, alongside the rooms set aside for his typists (lead by Miss Stenhouse), his Parliamentary Private Secretary, Brigadier Harvie-Watt, his personal adviser, Major Desmond Morton, his naval ADC, Commander Thompson and the Deputy Secretary to the Cabinet, Norman Brook. Immediately adjacent to the Churchills' dining room was Brendon Bracken's room. Bracken was one of Churchill's closest friends and his Minister of Information.

The Chiefs of Staff, the professional heads of the Army, Navy and Air Force, were given a large room in this complex. Original maps from the basement Map Room of the Admiralty now hang in this meeting room. These maps were used by Churchill during the first year of the war when he was First Lord of the Admiralty.

The Chiefs of Staff Conference Room

The Churchills' Private Rooms

Winston Churchill was very close to his wife and liked to have her nearby and be assured of her safety, and so a room was allocated to her in the basement HQ. It was a natural corollary to that to have a dining room for them both and Room 7 was set aside for this purpose. The dining table, sideboard and trolley are the very originals which were once part of the room.

Mrs Churchill's bedroom

The Churchills' Private Kitchen

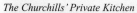

While there is no record of how many times the rooms of the Churchill Suite were used - or indeed if they were ever used by the occupants for whom they were intended - contemporary photographs show them fully fitted and furnished. These pictures were particularly valuable in putting the kitchen back together, though the search for two matching 1930s electric stoves (they did not have gas) identical to those used here was a challenge! The sink with its sump and pump (waste had to be hand cranked to the surface) were found in a neglected corner of the Treasury building and the plate warmer was given by The Duke of York from the effects of Windsor Lodge, home of the late Queen Elizabeth the Queen Mother.

Britain and the United States

The close link between Britain and the United States was being forged even before America entered the Second World War. From the very beginning of the war, many individual Americans offered practical help. Food parcels from the States lifted austerity from many British kitchens and the Americans opened their homes to child evacuees from Britain.

In March 1941 President Roosevelt signed the Lend-Lease Bill which enabled Britain to obtain supplies of all kinds from the United States and to defer payment until after the war. The Atlantic Charter, a joint declaration of principles, followed the first meetings between the British Prime Minister and the American President in August 1941.

Four months later, the United States were also at war with Japan and Germany. Between 1942 and the end of the war, over a million American troops served in Britain. Close co-operation between the national leaders was essential while Allied forces were fighting in North Africa, Italy and, from June 1944 onwards, under an American Supreme Commander in North-West Europe.

Winston Churchill recognised from the start of the war that the support of the United States was vital to an Allied victory and saw the relationship between the English-speaking powers on opposite sides of the Atlantic as a very special one. Addressing Congress in December 1941 Churchill drew parallels between American and British attitudes to the war. 'Here in Washington,' he said, 'I have found . . . an inflexible purpose and the proof of a sure and well-grounded confidence in the final outcome. We in Britain had the same feeling in our darkest days. We, too, were sure in the end all would be well. You do not, I am certain, underrate the severity of the ordeal to which you and we have still to be subjected. The forces ranged against us are enormous. They are bitter, they are ruthless . . . They will stop at nothing.'

He then built on this common purpose proclaiming that 'Now that we are together, now that we are linked in a righteous comradeship of arms, now that our two considerable nations, each in perfect unity, have joined all their life energies in a common resolve, a new scene opens upon which a steady light will glow and brighten.

'I avow my hope and faith, sure and inviolate, that in the days to come the British and American peoples will for their own safety and for the good of all walk together side by side in majesty, in justice and in peace.'

The President of the United States of America, Franklin Roosevelt, and the British Prime Minister, Winston Churchill, on board HMS Prince of Wales *in August 1941.* IWM H 12739

Life in the Corridor

While it has not been possible to show how intensely space in the corridor would have been used, most often by siting typists at the widest points, certain features of the area today still reflect the general shortage of space, as well as the continuance of daily life. The large map chests, which flank the doorway to the Map Room, housed most of the multitude of maps which were used to chart developments in the many theatres of war and which were constantly being shuffled around as events and the demands of the Joint Planning Staff required.

Just next to one of them can be seen the post box, where ordinary mail from the Rooms' occupants was deposited and from which it was collected four times daily. Incoming mail would be placed in the rack beside it.

Further evidence of the fears that troubled people in those times can be seen along this part of the corridor. The gas filters, located by signs painted on the wall, bear witness to the widespread notion in the 1930s that gas would be used as a weapon against cities, in the same way that it had rapidly become a feature of daily life on the Western Front in the First World War. The thick stubs of walls jutting out at intervals along the corridor were designed to limit the effective range of blast from a bomb or even an artillery shell and betray the constant concern that the enemy could attack in force at any time.

A Royal Marine orderly on duty at the wartime entrance to the Cabinet War Rooms, on the ground floor of the New Public Offices. PAUL POPPER

Plan chests, in which maps were stored, in the main Cabinet War Rooms corridor.

The two-metre thick protective 'slab' revealed.

At the hair-pin bend of the corridor lies Room 59, which once housed members of the Joint Planning Staff, comprising members of all three arms of the fighting forces. It was their role to assess the military situation and devise possible strategies for submission to the Chiefs of Staff and the Prime Minister himself. In 1942 this and adjoining rooms were made available to the enigmatic figure known only as 'C', the anonymous head of British Intelligence at that time, whose presence close to the heart of policy planning became increasingly necessary as the war progressed.

The room is now used to provide more detailed information about the site and to give a unique view of the massive reinforced surface under which the whole complex is sheltered. The cutaway cross-section at one end of the room shows the solid block of concrete that still covers the site. This slab is crudely strengthened with steel tramlines and rests on thick steel girders and wooden beams (to give flexibility in case of impact). The visitor leaves this area by a corridor which has been created to allow a new and intimate view of wartime life in the rooms.

The Threat of Invasion and British Civilian Morale

Throughout the summer of 1940 the large forces needed for Operation 'Sea Lion' – Hitler's plan to invade England – were being assembled on the French side of the Channel. In the meantime the Luftwaffe began the systematic bombing of British airfields, in an attempt to reduce the power of the Royal Air Force to oppose sea-borne landings along the south coast. Churchill described this crucial phase as the 'Battle of Britain' and the intense series of attacks and the heroic resistance to them were to mark one of the major turning points in the war. It was widely feared that the enemy would land on British shores. Behind the front line, last ditch defenders, such as the ill-equipped Home Guard, or 'Dad's Army' as it was nicknamed, were preparing to offer what resistance they could to battle-trained victorious German troops.

Looking back several decades later, it is clear that the German failure to defeat the RAF in the Battle of Britain made an effective invasion across the Channel in 1940 a practical impossibility. While the Battle of Britain was fought for supremacy in the air, the intense bombardment of British cities in 1940 and 1941 (the Blitz) was a prolonged attempt to crush civilian morale and destroy industries. At its most severe from September 1940 to May 1941, it caused destruction and casualties on a massive scale, with raids that, during the worst periods, seemed to follow each other day and night for weeks on end. Public shelters had been erected throughout the country in preparation for such an eventuality, and though they helped morale and gave some protection, not all could withstand a direct hit from a bomb.

Like the deeper London Underground stations that the public gradually occupied (despite initial Government attempts to stop this) these shelters became second homes to thousands. The scenes of devastation and personal loss that greeted people on surfacing after a raid sorely tested civilian morale, which had already been buffetted by deprivation and the fear that Britain would be the next step in Hitler's swift and apparently irresistible advance across Europe. Despite everything, public morale held firm and what passed into the English language as 'the Blitz spirit' bred a genuine sense of collective responsibility and mutual help amid random misfortune.

A sand bag pillbox being constructed outside the New Public Offices, spring 1940. IWM H 1584

With each new year of the war pressure on accommodation in the complex grew and most of the rooms that run off the main corridor had to be divided – and often sub-divided – to allow more and more personnel who were considered to be vital to particular aspects of the war effort to be housed.

The first small room, Room 60 Left, housed the outside broadcasting equipment which the BBC installed at the outbreak of war. This enabled the Prime Minister to speak to the people of Great Britain, the Commonwealth and occupied Europe, despite his being forced to shelter underground. Churchill, already renowned as an accomplished orator, exploited the convenience of having the facility to broadcast so close to hand and, in 1940–41, delivered four major speeches from his office-bedroom further along the corridor. These were then relayed from the equipment in Room 60 Left to the outside world.

BBC radio transmitting equipment in Room 60 Left.

Mr. Churchill, in his famous 'siren suit', broadcasting from No. 10 Downing Street. IWM H 20446

Room 60 Right

Switchboard operators at work in Room 60 Left in 1945. PAUL POPPER

Many of the rooms changed use as the situation required, but Room 60 Right, like a number of others, has been restored with the fittings which would have been found here in 1940 and 1941, when it was used as a telephone exchange for the complex and as an overspill – as so many areas were – for typing services. The increasing expansion of office accommodation further and further into the building at this level soon overloaded the inadequate switchboard and another, room-sized, switchboard was established on the left-hand side of the main corridor. Throughout the site staff worked shifts round the clock, and offices doubled up as bedrooms to ensure that personnel were immediately available at any time of day or night.

In many of the rooms are the essential accoutrements of everyday life in the war: the gas masks, which everyone carried almost as second nature; the helmets, which were a useful protection against possible flying debris or bomb splinters; and the whistle, would have been used to warn of fire in the Cabinet War Rooms.

Room 60A

Room 60A was, for a long time, occupied by the typing pool and was busy twenty-four hours a day, particularly following the late night meetings of the Cabinet and the Chiefs of Staff. The typists had also to meet the heavy demands of the ever-increasing numbers of Joint Planning Staff who occupied more and more rooms in the basement.

Accurate minutes and reports had to be typed up, with two carbon copies, and made available for circulation within a matter of hours, regardless of the time of day or night. In an age of word processors and photocopiers, the equipment, particularly the Gestetner ink stencil copier in the middle of the room, may seem archaic and the arduous job of producing pristine documents, with only an eraser to help correct mistakes, now seems almost impossible. At least some effort was made to ease the problems caused by working for long hours without ever seeing daylight and staff were given regular ultra-violet treatment.

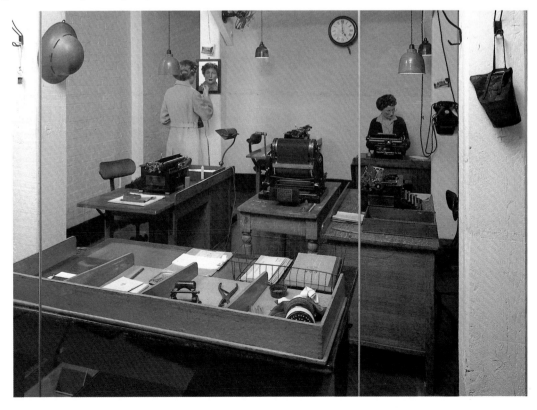

The typing pool, Room 60A.

Office Workers in the Cabinet War Rooms

'I used to spend every other night sleeping in the office . . . sometimes I was there for about three nights running, because I just couldn't get home, so in some ways I was fortunate that even in this revolting place called 'the dock' one could get a good night's sleep, because you didn't hear the bombs raining down, which is just as well, because we'd have all been buried alive in the Cabinet War Rooms.'

Betty Green
Personal Secretary to General Ismay

Second World War gas mask issued to all civilians in Britain.

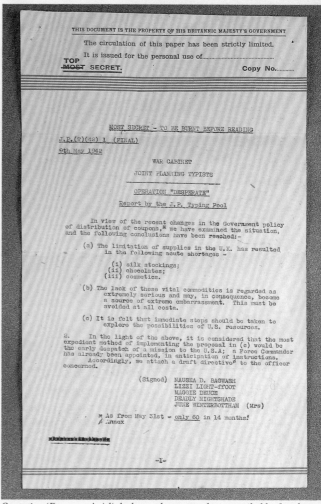

THIS DOCUMENT IS THE PROPERTY OF HIS BRITANNIC MAJESTY'S GOVERNMENT

The circulation of this paper has been strictly limited.

It is issued for the personal use of..............................

TOP ~~MOST~~ SECRET.   Copy No...........

MOST SECRET – TO BE BURNT BEFORE READING

J.P.(T)(42) 1 (FINAL)
9th May 1942

WAR CABINET

JOINT PLANNING TYPISTS

OPERATION "DESPERATE"

Report by the J.P. Typing Pool

In view of the recent changes in the Government policy of distribution of coupons,* we have examined the situation, and the following conclusions have been reached:-

(a) The limitation of supplies in the U.K. has resulted in the following acute shortages –

   (i) silk stockings;
   (ii) chocolates;
   (iii) cosmetics.

(b) The lack of these vital commodities is regarded as extremely serious and may, in consequence, become a source of extreme embarrassment. This must be avoided at all costs.

(c) It is felt that immediate steps should be taken to explore the possibilities of U.S. resources.

2. In the light of the above, it is considered that the most expedient method of implementing the proposal in (c) would be the early despatch of a mission to the U.S.A; a Force Commander has already been appointed, in anticipation of instructions. Accordingly, we attach a draft directive* to the officer concerned.

(Signed) NAUSEA D. BAGWASH
LIZZI LIGHT-ffOOT
MAGGIE DEUCE
DEADLY NIGHTSHADE
JUNE WINTERBOTTHAM (Mrs)

* As from May 31st – only 60 in 14 months!
β Annex

-1-

Junior members of the Military Secretariat from the Cabinet War Rooms in the Crimea during the Yalta conference, 1945.
(Photo courtesy the Hon. Mrs. SUSAN EVETTS)

Operation 'Desperate'. A light-hearted memorandum compiled by female staff of the Cabinet War Rooms in 1942. (Operation 'Desperate' was a complete success.)

General Hollis and the Cabinet War Rooms secretaries at the Potsdam Conference in 1945.
Left to right: *Miss Christopher, General Hollis, Miss Sutherland, Miss Umney-Gray.*
IWM HU 44888

Churchill and his secretaries

'He did not mean to be unkind. He was just heart and soul engaged in winning the war.'

So wrote one of Churchill's private secretaries, Elizabeth Nel, in a memoir which abounds with similar 'excuses' for the fierce temper for which her employer was renowned. Churchill was a severe taskmaster, who frequently lost patience with his personal secretaries and typists, while obliging them to work well past midnight, after hours of mumbled dictation, interspersed with demands for instant and precise recall of something he had said numerous pages before. It is an accusation sometimes made against this workaholic, for whom day and night seemed to have little distinction, that he showed a lack of understanding of the difficulties of the daily lives of those who worked for him.

One of his secretaries, Miss Shearburn, recalls, how, on one occasion, Churchill finally ended a particularly long and arduous session of composing and dictating a vital speech at 3.00 am with the casual remark 'Don't bother with a fair copy of that tonight . . . I shan't want it until eight o'clock'. But all of those who worked with him voice unstinting praise for this man who thought nothing of giving dictation anywhere, even in a state of semi-undress, and frequently reduced his female staff to tears with his rudeness, incited by some failure to spell correctly his unintelligible delivery of a foreign name.

Often his secretaries did not bother with shorthand note taking and typed straight from the Prime Minister's dictation. This might reasonably explain his infamous dislike of the noise of typewriters which led to the custom-made 'silent' typewriters, examples of which were kept at all of his regular working locations.

Air raid precautions: a whistle and a helmet hang ready for use in the typing pool.

Rooms 61 Left and 61 Right

This already small room, number 61, was partitioned early in the war in order to provide, in 61 Left, both emergency office and bedroom space for Commander Maurice Knott RN (known by all as 'Senior') and Lieutenant-Commander Ian McEwan RNVR (inevitably known as 'Junior'), the two Private Secretaries of General Sir Hastings Ismay. 61 Right was reserved for Ismay himself, for whom, as Chief of Staff to Churchill and as Deputy Secretary to the Cabinet, close proximity to the Prime Minister was vital.

However, in common with other senior staff in the War Rooms, Ismay also had accommodation on one of the upper floors of the building above. He used his under-ground office and bedroom principally when the bombing raids were at their worst or when Churchill's habit of holding late night meetings, ending well into the early hours, made the prospect of scaling several flights of stairs even less inviting than sleeping underground with electric fans and noisy ventilation.

The war, and life in a cramped underground shelter with few comforts and long hours of work bred a spirit of common cause, but it is interesting to note the obvious differences between the Secretary's room and that of his superior: the desk, lamp, size of bed and, above all, carpet, delineate the difference in rank. Despite the relatively Spartan appearance of the rooms, the accommodation they offered was far superior to that which so many had to suffer in the 'dock'.

In each of these rooms, as in many others, a small panel of three knobs connected by a wire leading upwards to the ceiling enabled senior staff to summon their juniors at the press of a button. Connections led to Winston Churchill's suite of offices and to the Cabinet Room itself.

Hastings Ismay

General Sir Hastings Ismay (later Lord Ismay).
Photo courtesy the Hon. Mrs. SUSAN EVETTS

Hastings Ismay was a professional soldier whose outstanding career before 1940 fitted him perfectly for the crucial role he was to play as Churchill's personal representative on the Chiefs of Staff Committee. Having joined the 21st Cavalry Regiment of the Indian Army in 1907, he was seconded to the Somaliland Camel Corps and served with distinction in Somaliland throughout the First World War. Between the wars Ismay returned to India where his brilliance as a staff officer led, in 1938, to his appointment as Secretary to the Committee of Imperial Defence.

Known affectionately as 'Pug', Ismay was the lynch-pin between the often irascible and self-willed Churchill and his senior military commanders. During the Second World War, as Deputy Secretary (Military) to the Cabinet and Chief of Staff to Churchill as Minister of Defence, it fell to Ismay to deal with all military matters arising from Cabinet meetings and to be the main link between the Prime Minister and the heads of the Army, Navy and Air Force. He served Churchill faithfully until 1945 and subsequently continued in office under the Labour Prime Minister, Clement Attlee, retiring from the Army in 1946.

Among all who worked with him he was justly famed and universally respected for his apparently limitless patience. Even this was tested to the limit in September 1944 by Churchill's temper and, for the only time in the war, Ismay threatened to resign. His profound respect for Churchill led him to withdraw his threat, but he continued to hold true to his avowed principle that 'if once I said "Yes" when I thought "No", I would be no more use to him.'

Like so many outstanding staff officers, his was never to become a household name, though his achievements, not least as Chairman of the Festival of Britain in 1951 and, from 1951 to 1957, as the first Secretary-General of NATO, deserve greater acclaim. One who did recognise Ismay's qualities, General (later President) Eisenhower, wrote of him that he was the 'greatest of modern British soldiers, but at the same time the least recognised'.

Ismay retired completely in 1957 and died in 1965, just months after Winston Churchill.

Rooms 61A Left and 61A Right

As in the two previous rooms, Rooms 61A Left and Right were allocated to one of the most senior persons under Churchill on the site, and his Private Secretaries.

In this case 61A Right belonged to Sir Edward Bridges, who held the post of Secretary to the Cabinet and, as the most senior civil servant in the country, actioned civil and political matters discussed by the Cabinet. Though Bridges was a more reserved and less flamboyant person than Ismay, together they achieved a harmonious and ultimately efficient working method. This allowed the Cabinet to function smoothly and allowed its decisions to be channelled quickly to the many individuals whose job it was to put them into effect immediately.

Once again the differences in rank between the senior man and his assistants are marked by different levels of comfort in the austere surroundings of the War Rooms. Unlike Ismay, Edward Bridges often actually preferred to sleep in his underground room, particularly when the Blitz was at its height.

Sir Edward Bridges (later Lord Bridges).
Photo courtesy ROBERT BRIDGES Esq.

A combined office and bedroom, Room 61A Right.

Alan Brooke

General Alan Brooke (later Field Marshal Lord Alanbrooke).
IWM H 15522

Alan Brooke was commissioned into the Royal Artillery in 1902, and served for four years on the Western Front during the First World War. The inter-war years gave him a firm grounding in staff work, but he remained through-out his life an accomplished and keen active soldier. He demonstrated his outstanding military skill with his command of II Corps of the British Expeditionary Force in France in 1940, where he has been credited with having saved the British forces from total destruction.

His success there led to his appointment as Commander-in-Chief Home Forces, with responsibility for the defence of the country against the anticipated German invasion. In 1941, when the threat of invasion had receded, Brooke was Churchill's personal choice as Chief of the Imperial General Staff and subsequently as Chairman of the Chiefs of Staff Committee.

His reputation as CIGS was as an efficient, cool-headed and self-disciplined leader and his achievements in directing this previously loosely defined body have been recognised by contemporaries and historians alike. However, his personal diaries reveal a man of modest ambition and minimal conceit, unnerved by the 'dizzy heights' of the position of CIGS, 'looking out on to a landscape . . . bleak and lonely, with a ghastly responsibility hanging as a black thundercloud.'

In August 1942 he was tempted by Churchill's offer of command of the British Forces Middle East – the field command he had yearned for and an opportunity to play a major role in 'turning the tide of the war'. Despite this, he declined the post, believing that he could give his country greater service by continuing to exercise his finely tuned skill in tempering the Prime Minister's 'impetuous nature, his gambler's spirit, and his determination to follow his own selected path at all costs.' He added ruefully: 'there is no doubt in my mind that Winston never realised what this decision cost me.'

In a personal tribute to Churchill, after he had been voted out of office in July 1945, Alanbrooke, who had worked closer to him than anyone else – and had suffered more from his ire than most – thanked God for the 'opportunity of working alongside such a man, and of having my eyes opened to the fact that such supermen exist on this earth.'

Brooke continued to serve as CIGS until he retired in January 1946, having been ennobled as Viscount Alanbrooke, and died in June 1963.

Instructions for escape in emergency.

Rooms 62 and 62A

For the crucial months of July 1940 to January 1941, which saw some of the heaviest and most frequent air attacks of the war on Great Britain, Rooms 62 and 62A constituted the Advanced Headquarters of the GHQ Home Forces. Put simply, from these two rooms, among these basic schoolroom-like furnishings, the whole defence of the country against enemy air attack and the threat of invasion was to be organised in the event of an invasion.

General Headquarters Home Forces was established in the spring of 1940 and given premises some miles away in the west of London. As the German *Blitzkrieg* made its rapid advance across Europe the importance of GHQ Home Forces became paramount. The Chiefs of Staff pressed for this important organisation to be accommodated in the Cabinet War Rooms, with immediate access to the Prime Minister, and Rooms 62 and 62A were given over to the junior and senior staff, respectively.

A telephone with a warning on its dial, Room 62.

The Cabinet War Rooms standing instructions gave precise details of emergency procedures, particularly in the event of a gas attack or German troops besieging the site. On them lies a hole puncher. Churchill insisted that every document which came before him should be punched and tagged, not clipped or pinned.

Rooms 62B and 63

Room 62B was allocated to the Commander-in-Chief of Home Forces, General Sir Alan Brooke (later to become Field Marshal Lord Alanbrooke) in 1940.

From 1941 onwards it was the office of the so-called 'Camp Commandant'. This post was held from 1943 until the end of the war by Lawrence Burgis, who was also Assistant Secretary to the War Cabinet. He was responsible for the upkeep, supply, maintenance and security of the site on a day to day basis and, for this reason, the door leading into Room 62B is cluttered with the original keys which gave full or restricted access to all the rooms of the complex.

When in use the room would have been full of office furniture and telephones, crowded around the rough wooden props which were such a feature of the site from its earliest days. This simple measure of reinforcement might seem derisory but the fortification which confronts the visitor on leaving this room for what was once Room 63 is much more impressive.

A marine sentry with the keys to the Cabinet War Rooms, Room 62B.
IWM HU 44277

The Tunnel

Towards the end of 1941 it was realised that the staircase in the building above was situated directly over this room, which in turn lay immediately adjacent to the vital Map Rooms, and it was thought that a bomb hitting the building could easily cause a serious structural collapse at this point. To prevent this, the Camp Commandant was relocated next door and the simple expedient followed of filling the room with solid concrete, to a thickness of five metres in every direction.

To enable visitors to walk through to the Map Rooms it was necessary to drill a channel through this concrete block, a task which took some three months to complete, using diamond tipped drills.

The Map Room Annexe

The visitor emerges at the far end of the tunnel into a narrow passage surrounded by a mixture of strange objects and confronted by a huge map of Europe covered in coloured pins and long tracks of thin woollen thread. This room was used for the overspill from the Map Room proper and gave a little extra space to the planners who analysed and reported on the war for the Prime Minister and the military chiefs, using what to us seem like the most primitive and labour intensive methods.

To the right is a stereoscope, a device used for viewing aerial pictures. Two identical images were placed alongside one another, and the device gave them a three dimensional appearance, enabling the specialist analysts to distinguish different features of landscapes and cities which were to be bombed or were being studied to establish how effective bombing attacks had been.

To the left of the exit from the tunnel is one of the American 'Frigidaire' air-conditioning machines used to supplement the heavily over-worked central system.

The map which so dominates this little room spent most of the war on one of the walls of the main Map Room next door and charts in great detail the devastating advance of the German forces in Russia in 1941–42 and their gradual retreat in the years that followed. One can imagine those who worked here documenting the depressing daily advances made by Hitler's armies across a major portion of the map of continental Europe and feel their relief at finally seeing ever-growing signs of a turn in the tide. The map also marks the boundaries which were imposed on eastern Europe in 1945. The fact that it was kept for planning the Allied occupation of western Europe after the end of the war serves as a reminder that, at that time, there was a widespread fear that the end of one war with one enemy might mark the start of another war with a former ally.

This map illustrates better than anything else in the Rooms the scale and complex nature of the restoration work carried out in the early 1980s. Every detail had to be carefully photographed, each pin and woollen thread gingerly removed, and each sheet professionally conserved, before being replaced in their previous positions.

The tunnel, drilled through solid concrete, leading to the Map Room Annexe.

Another feature of the crowded Map Room Annexe is, on the right, the telephone switch frame which enabled officers to make secure calls from their own rooms, sharing a single scrambler device. Further along the same wall are charts drawn up by Map Room officers which detail the number of V-1s fired on the south of England in 1944.

The V-Weapons

Only a week after the Allied invasion of German occupied France in June 1944 Hitler's final 'wonder weapons' were unleashed on Great Britain.

The *Vergeltungswaffen* or 'vengeance weapons' had been under development for several years and the first of them, the V-1, was a twenty-five foot jet propelled missile, fitted with wings sixteen feet wide. In Britain V-1s were rapidly nicknamed 'Doodlebugs' or 'Buzz Bombs'. They were fired from fixed ramps, that were quickly erected at various locations in Northern France, or, when the Allies overran these, from the underside of modified Heinkel bombers. Each missile carried a one-ton warhead up to 250 miles at speeds of about 400 miles an hour and, when its engine cut out, it glided at an angle towards its target.

Those on the ground could see them flying through the air and observe their sharp descent, but could not know with any degree of accuracy just where they would land. Their impact was devastating, wiping out whole buildings or streets at one blow and their sudden arrival, just as the war seemed to be going so well, was profoundly demoralising. The charts on the Map Room Annexe wall show in precise detail the vast numbers of these weapons which were targeted at England in the summer and autumn of 1944, as well as the terrible number of casualties they caused. With the use of improved equipment, and with practice, V-1s were increasingly intercepted in flight.

The same charts show how many of the V-1s were destroyed by Allied fighter aircraft, radar controlled anti-aircraft fire and by barrage balloons. These means of defence, however, were ineffective against the second of Hitler's V-weapons, the V-2 rocket, of which 5,000 were launched against London from elusive mobile carriers between September 1944 and 27 March 1945, before Allied bomber aircraft finally managed to knock out their research, production and storage sites.

The V-2 was a forty-six-foot rocket, weighing thirteen tons and carrying a one-ton warhead. Flying at a speed of 3,500 feet per second, its arrival came without any forewarning, though its impact was reduced because it exploded after its enormous velocity had propelled it deep into the ground. London was not the only target of these weapons and other cities such as Antwerp in liberated Belgium suffered heavily as a result of V-2 raids.

Left: *V-1 flying bomb crashing towards a street off Drury Lane, London, in July 1944.* IWM HU 636

Below: *Cabinet War Rooms staff compiled this table relating to the first two months of V-1 attacks in 1944.*

FLYING BOMBS

24 HRS ENDED 0600	PLOTT'D	OVER COAST	OVER LONDON	DESTROYED				CASUALTIES		
				FTRS	AA	BLNS	TOTAL	FATAL	SERIOUS	SL'T
								To 9-8-44.		
TOTALS FR'M 16.6.44 TO 22.8.44 INCL'SVE	7369	5074	2359	1850	291	259	3400	4918	14625	

The Map Room

The Map Room came into use on the very first day that the Cabinet War Rooms were ready for occupation and never ceased to be the hub of the whole site until V J Day. Quietly closed down the next day, 16 August 1945, it was left almost exactly as we see it today, every book, map, chart, pin and notice occupying the same position now that they occupied then.

The large map by the entrance hangs where it hung for most of the war. It illustrates the routes taken by the many convoys which crossed the open wastes of a submarine-infested Atlantic, which froze in the sub-zero temperatures of the sea lanes to North Russia, or ran the gauntlet of the Mediterranean to collect and deliver vital supplies, food and matériel for Great Britain, its allies and its forces fighting overseas. The many thousands of tiny dots which cloud the surface of the map are pinholes left by markers shifted around by the map keepers, as each convoy steamed towards its destination or was decimated *en route* by enemy torpedoes.

Entry to the Map Room was strictly limited. This list of those permitted to enter is now pinned to the door of the Map Room Annexe.

Part of the Convoy Map in the Map Room.

The colourful array of telephones, nicknamed 'the beauty chorus' by those who worked in the Map Room.

On other walls are pasted large scale maps of the seas around the United Kingdom and of the Far Eastern theatres of war, showing the lines held by the Allies as the war there drew to a close. This latter map, which was fixed in place during the later period of the war, also shows the massive scale of the island-hopping operations by the American sea-borne forces in the Pacific in their campaign to winkle out enemy troops that threatened them at every turn.

The blackboard which hangs on the pillar towards one end of the room was used during the Battle of Britain to note the numbers of enemy aircraft destroyed each day. A member of the map room staff is thought to have painted in the details, as they were known then, of the successes and casualties of 15 September 1940, the day which came to be known as Battle of Britain Day and which marked the turning point in the struggle to resist the intended invasion. It was on this day that Churchill, who had witnessed the aerial dogfights from the ground at No. 11 Group Headquarters at RAF Uxbridge, neatly summed up the situation with the words: 'The odds were great; our margins small; the stakes infinite'.

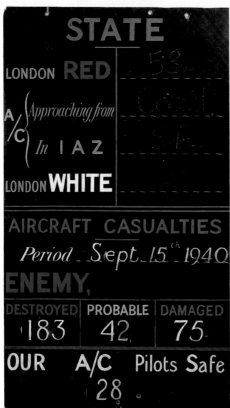

Blackboard showing the tally of aircraft believed to have been shot down on 'Battle of Britain Day', 15 September 1940.

Life in the Map Room

Map Room equipment including (on the left) the Lanson tubes through which message capsules were propelled by compressed air.

Throughout the war the long table in the centre of the Map Room was in constant use. At it would be seated five officers, brought out of retirement to help in the war effort. One member each of the Royal Navy, the Royal Air Force, the Army and the Ministry of Home Security occupied specific positions, while another, selected from each service in turn, took the end seat and served as Duty Officer. Around the edges of the room, plotters would be moving pins on maps fixed to the walls or to the movable partitions to the right of the entrance doorway. Meanwhile telephones were ringing – at the busiest periods of the war, almost constantly – with news of the most recent developments. Whatever the news, whether glorious or disastrous, the mood was always one of unruffled calm efficiency.

Using a particular colour of telephone, the officers on duty could communicate with intelligence sources (via the green telephones – those with green handsets had a 'scramble' facility), or another service war room (the white telephones), or be connected to their switchboard (the black telephones). It was their job to filter through a welter of incoming up-dates on the war's progress on land, sea and in the air, to plot the changes on the many maps which were readily to hand and to compile daily reports for transmission every morning to the Prime Minister, the Chiefs of Staff and to the King at Buckingham Palace. Communication with the Prime Minister was maintained

The Duty Officer's place at the Map Room's central table.

via the ivory coloured telephone at the end of the table nearest to the Duty Officer, which provided a direct line to Number 10 Downing Street. Churchill, who was obsessed with maps and the need to chart events on them, was a frequent visitor to this nerve centre of the complex.

Another major means of communication was introduced by the General Post Office in February 1940: the vacuum message tube. A capsule containing a document would be inserted into one of the thick brass tubes, which can be seen running into the floor in the centre of the room and across the ceiling at the other end, and, in seconds, would be propelled by compressed air to the Air Ministry's own underground headquarters at the far end of the building.

Access to the Map Room was strictly controlled. Among the very few who were privileged to be allowed in occasionally were a number of visiting heads of Allied countries or of their armed forces. The King and Queen themselves came to the Map Room in May 1942, and were followed some time later by General Eisenhower, the Supreme Commander, Allied Expeditionary Force accompanied by a retinue which included Generals Spaatz and Grueber.

Those Allied overseas statesmen and military leaders granted access to the Map Room gained not only an up to date insight into the progress of the war, but also experienced the modern nature of Churchill's 'nerve centre'. This boasted such novel features as full air conditioning (the same equipment is still operational – though the fixtures have been discreetly modernised – to this day), neon lighting and, on the pillar next to the Duty Officer's table, an ingenious cigarette lighter that used a bell push and a glowing piece of fuse wire to keep the area relatively flame free.

Elizabeth Nel, a wartime secretary to Churchill, wrote in her memoirs that she sometimes resented the 'Map Room boys': 'They didn't work particularly hard,' she complained. 'They oozed glamour and success and they managed to be in on every damn thing that was going'. Clearly those who worked in this room seem to have enjoyed a certain prestige, although they were not necessarily universally popular as a result.

Map Room officers on duty, May 1945. IWM MH 27688

Winston Churchill's Room

Churchill was not a man who shirked risks, indeed, if anything, his career and his actions demonstrate the opposite. His penchant for taking up position on the roof at George Street to gain a better view of the air attacks, and his many high-risk trips by plane or ship to meet other world leaders are legendary.

Although his room in the basement boasted comforts of a higher standard than anywhere else in the complex he preferred not to sleep there. However, he was occasionally obliged to spend the night there, when his military advisers and his personal detectives, who accompanied him wherever he went, successfully persuaded him that the man in whom the nation rested its hopes could not risk his life so freely by returning to his official residence.

Churchill continued to live and work above ground in Number 10 Downing Street until late in 1940 when he had alternative headquarters established on the first floor of the building above the Cabinet War Rooms. Here he had living, sleeping and office accommodation and a small 'map room' which his personal map keeper, Captain Richard Pim RNVR, used to keep him abreast of developments. This suite of rooms came to be known as 'Number 10 Annexe'.

The Prime Minister appreciated the value of the War Rooms. He insisted on having as close access as possible to the Map Room and his office was sited right next door to it, with a communicating door. On four occasions during the dark days of the second half of 1940, after the majority of central Europe had fallen to Hitler's armies, it was from this office, that Churchill spoke via the BBC to the nations of the world and stirred their citizens with his trenchant words and unrelenting spirit.

Here too he met the Heads of State, the politicians and military figures who visited the Map Room, although the curtains by the wall maps in his room, on which are marked the country's coastal defences, as well as the possible landing points for a potential German invasion, might be discreetly pulled across.

The Prime Minister's bed – night shirt on pillow, emergency lighting to hand.

Churchill's desk in his office-bedroom in the Cabinet War Rooms. The microphones provided by the BBC for his broadcasts to the world stand at one end.

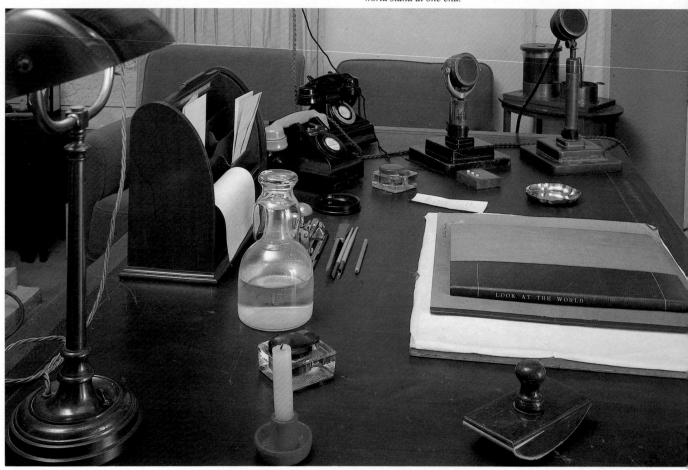

Winston Churchill

Churchill in characteristic ebullient pose, September 1940. <small>CECIL BEATON</small>

Sir Winston Leonard Spencer Churchill
1874–1965

30 November 1874	Born at Bleinheim Palace
1888–1892	Pupil at Harrow School
February 1895	Second Lieutenant with 4th Hussars
1899–1900	War correspondent for Morning Post during South African war, taken prisoner, escaped.
October 1900	Elected Conservative Member of Parliament for Oldham
May 1904	Joins Liberal Party
December 1905	Under-Secretary of State at Colonial Office
January 1906	Elected Liberal MP for North-West Manchester
1908–1910	President of the Board of Trade
April 1908	Defeated in North-West Manchester by-election
May 1908	Elected Liberal MP for Dundee
12 September 1908	Marries Clementine Hozier
1910–1911	Home Secretary
1911–1915	First Lord of the Admiralty
November 1915– May 1916	Serves in France with the Royal Scots Fusiliers
1917–1918	Minister of Munitions
1919–1921	Secretary of State for War
1921–1922	Secretary of State for the Colonies
1922–1924	Out of Parliament
October 1924	Elected Constitutionalist– Conservative MP for Epping
1924–1929	Chancellor of the Exchequer
September 1939– May 1940	First Lord of the Admiralty
May 1940– July 1945	Prime Minister
July 1945– October 1951	Leader of the Opposition
October 1951– April 1955	Prime Minister
24 January 1965	Died, buried at Bladon, Oxfordshire

Churchill's daily routine

Those who worked closely with Churchill as Prime Minister during the war recount a daily routine that scarcely changed, regardless of whether he was ensconced in Number 10 Downing Street, sheltering in the Cabinet War Rooms or on a visit to see President Roosevelt in the United States.

He would regularly awake at about 8.30 am, have a cigar in bed, the first of about a dozen that day – lit from a candle which was always kept nearby and extinguished for him by his secretary – and would then hold court, sitting propped up in bed, wearing his green and gold dressing gown with its dragon motif decoration. He would read all the major daily newspapers, study the thick pile of papers in his Prime Ministerial box, give dictation to his secretaries, send his Private Secretaries running to deliver various documents, and hold discussions with senior military advisers, who would regularly include Alanbrooke and Ismay. A soak in his tub would take place mid-way through the morning, but would in no way interrupt proceedings.

Meal times were seldom changed and both lunch and dinner would be accompanied by champagne. A mid-afternoon nap, followed by a bath were habits adhered to in even the most unlikely circumstances, but probably gave Churchill his legendary ability to work until 3.00 or 4.00 a m, totally oblivious, as his wartime Private Secretary, Sir John Colville, tells us, to the fatigue or hunger of those around him. Much to the chagrin of his hard-worked Chiefs of Staff, who might have subsequent meetings on matters arising, he would sometimes call a Cabinet meeting at 11.00 or 12.00 at night.

Despite his famed lack of patience, his impetuosity, his sarcasm and above all his anger, those who worked under Churchill, from his valet to his CIGS, fell under his spell. They recognised his genius, as well as his genuine affection and support for friends and all who had served him. They tolerated his fire, which was quite often extinguished seconds later by a gentle smile or a kind word.

Churchill's Private Office Staff (Rooms 66 to 68)

The rooms which come between Churchill's office and the Cabinet Room all form part of what was once the sequence of steps to a meeting with the Prime Minister, though today's visitor retraces them in reverse order.

The Prime Minister's visitors would have passed through the hands of his Principal Private Secretary, John Martin, in Room 66B or met with other members of his Private Office in Rooms 66A or 67. Room 68 was a waiting room.

The first of these rooms, Room 66, is now used for temporary exhibitions relating to different aspects of the history of the Second World War.

The narrow little room known as 66A houses a permanent display of firearms which once belonged to Sir Winston Churchill. Most prominent among these is Churchill's Colt .45 which he purchased when he left politics temporarily to serve on the Western Front in 1915. The weapon is inscribed with his name and was said by Inspector Thompson, the detective from Scotland Yard who was his principal protection officer for many years,

The Prime Minister with members of his staff. IWM HU 46095

Mr. Churchill inspecting a 'Tommy' gun, 31 July 1940.
IWM H 2646A

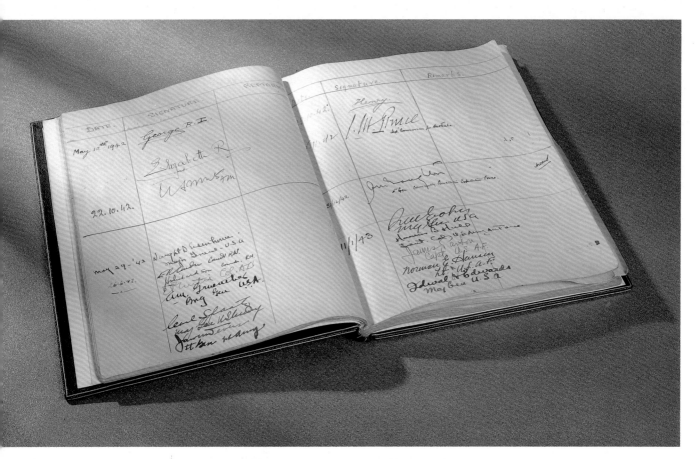

The Map Room visitors' book.

to have been Churchill's favourite gun. Thompson was ordered to carry the gun on his person ready for the Prime Minister's use throughout the Second World War.

Alongside is a photograph of Winston Churchill taken during a visit to the north east of England in 1940. In it he is carrying a Thompson sub-machine gun, and is wearing a pin-striped suit, a bow tie, a Homburg hat and is smoking a cigar. It is unlikely that the photographer had any inkling of the impact the picture was to have. The Prime Minister's style of dress was distinctive, but not untypical of the day. However the addition of the 'Tommy gun' suddenly gave him the appearance of a gangster, and, as a result, the picture was to feature prominently in enemy propaganda.

Room 67 is now home to a number of remarkable caricatures by the prolific cartoonist, Ralph Sallon. Having arrived in England as a Polish emigre before the First World War, Sallon soon made a name for himself as a keen observer of the famous and infamous and was one of the finest satirists of his time.

The Cabinet War Rooms Shop now occupies the room which functioned for most of the war as an officers' mess room, when it supplied basic snacks and drinks and gave some respite from the tensions of life at the crux of political and military planning.

The officers are gone now, along with the great Prime Minister, the marine garrison, the politicians and civil servants who once crowded the corridors and little offices of the Cabinet War Rooms. But their haunts remain and have helped, we hope, to bring alive for you some of the darkest yet most inspiring days of Britain's history.

George Rance in the Cabinet War Rooms mess room, 1945.
IWM HU 43874

General Information

Opening Hours and Admission

Open every day except 24 to 26 December, from 9.30 am (10.00 am from October to March) to 6.00 pm; last admissions 5.15 pm.

Admission fee charged. Reductions available for students, disabled persons, pensioners and unemployed, and for groups of 10 or more visitors. Children (up to 16 years old) free of charge.

Sound Guide

A personal audio guide is offered free of charge to every visitor and provides a multi-layered insight into the story of the Cabinet War Rooms. It is available in English, Dutch, French, German, Italian, Spanish, Hebrew and Swedish. A version especially designed for younger children is also available, but in English only.

Friends of the Imperial War Museum

In addition to the public free admission to the branches in London and the North, the Friends have free admission to the Cabinet War Rooms and HMS *Belfast* in London, and Imperial War Museum Duxford, near Cambridge, with the exception of special events at Duxford. Further benefits include the magazine of the society of Friends, special events and discounts in all the museum shops and cafes. Membership details from the Friends' Office, Imperial War Museum, Lambeth Road, London, SE1 6HZ. Tel: 020 7416 5255 or visit www.iwm.org.uk

Improving our Service

The Imperial War Museum aims for the highest possible standards of customer service at the Cabinet War Rooms.

You are invited to submit complaints, comments or suggestions for improvements to the Director, Cabinet War Rooms, Clive Steps, King Charles Street, London, SW1A 2AQ. Tel: 020 7930 6961. E-mail: cwr@iwm.org.uk

Shopping and Mail Order

A wide range of publications including books, audio visual material, postcards and educational resources are available from the Cabinet War Rooms gift shop and through a worldwide mail order service, along with a selection of gifts and souvenirs for all the family.

For a free mail order catalogue please write to: The Mail Department, Imperial War Museum, Duxford Airfield, Cambridge CB2 4QR.

Tel: 01223 499345 (24hr answer phone) or fax: 01223 839688.

E-mail: mailorder@iwm.org.uk

Café

The Switchroom cafeteria is a great place to relax. Offering a range of freshly prepared hot and cold food, along with a variety of beverages, it is open 7 days a week from 10.00 am until 5.00 pm. The cafeteria is located halfway through the tour, but visits to the cafeteria can be made at any time. Originally the switchroom during the wartime operation of the site, the cafeteria now also displays interesting photographs and images from the Second World War.

Education

The Cabinet War Rooms have recently created a brand new learning facility. The Clore Education centre boasts sophisticated systems for presentation and interactive work, including a computer suite and video conferencing facilities.

The Education team at the Cabinet War Rooms offer teaching sessions, free of charge, to all age groups and nationalities, on a wide variety of subjects. Teaching is customised to the needs of each individual group; sessions include slide and film presentations, use of the extensive hands-on collection of period artefacts, interactive workshops and group discussions.

If you would like to arrange a teaching session for your group, please call Mrs Jo Hunt on 020 7766 0132 or email jhunt@iwm.org.uk

Corporate and Private Hire

The Cabinet War Rooms has an auditorium with flexible seating for up to 140 people, and a smaller presentation space for up to 80. Both rooms have air conditioning and provide ultra-modern audio-visual equipment in a truly historic period setting. These spaces are available for hire throughout the day and for evening functions.

On site catering - from snacks and lunches to canapé receptions and elegant dinners - can be arranged through our exclusive caterer, Sodexho Prestige.

For further information or to make a booking, please call 020 7766 0134 or email cwr@sodexho-uk.com

Photographic portrait of Churchill by Yousuf Karsh

Future Plans

The restoration of the 'Churchill Suite' was the first part of a £13 million project to expand the Cabinet War Rooms, reinstating extensive secret areas which have never before been publicly accessible. The £7.5 million first phase of the expansion was achieved as a result of the generosity of the National Heritage Memorial Fund, which provided £2 million, and major contributions from The Clore Duffield Foundation and The Wolfson Foundation.

The second and final stage of the expansion project is the creation of the very first museum in this country dedicated to the life, achievements and legacy of '*the greatest Briton ever*', **Sir Winston Churchill**, at the Cabinet War Rooms, the scene of his 'finest hour'.

The museum will cost £6 million and will open here in January 2005, marking the fortieth anniversary of Sir Winston's death. It will include interactive and other high tech displays, as well as iconic objects, pictures and documents.

"Sail on, Oh Ship of State!

Sail on, Oh Union strong and great.

Humanity with all its fears

With all the hope of future years

Is hanging breathless on thy fate."

Franklin D Roosevelt to Winston Churchill, 20 January 1941

Funding

The Cabinet War Rooms receive almost no public subsidy and are required to be financially self-sufficient. To achieve the Churchill Museum we are dependent on donations from private individuals, trusts and corporations.

If you would like to make a donation towards this great heritage project, please do not hesitate to contact me. Anyone wishing to make a donation should make cheques payable to the *Imperial War Museum.*

The Project is represented in the USA by *The American Friends of the Churchill Museum*, an incorporated body with the IRS 501 (C) (3) not-for-profit tax exemption status. American nationals may make cheques payable to:

The American Friends of the Churchill Museum

PO Box 33028

Hartford CT

06150-3028

I hope you enjoyed your visit to the Cabinet War Rooms, that you re-visit soon and that you will come back in 2005 to see the Winston Churchill Museum. I am grateful to you for your support.

Phil Reed

Director, Cabinet War Rooms

Tel: 020 7766 0122

preed@iwm.org.uk